Ulla Universe

Janet Snyder and Kathleen Canova

Published by
Hasmark Publishing International
www.hasmarkpublishing.com

Copyright © 2024 Janet Snyder & Kathleen Canova

First Edition

No part of this book may be reproduced or transmitted in any form or by any means, electronic or mechanical, including photocopying, recording or by any information storage and retrieval system, without written permission from the author, except for the inclusion of brief quotations in a review.

Disclaimer:
This book is designed to provide information and motivation to our readers. It is sold with the understanding that the publisher is not engaged to render any type of psychological, legal, or any other kind of professional advice. The content of each article is the sole expression and opinion of its author, and not necessarily that of the publisher. No warranties or guarantees are expressed or implied by the publisher's choice to include any of the content in this volume. Neither the publisher nor the individual author(s) shall be liable for any physical, psychological, emotional, financial, or commercial damages, including, but not limited to, special, incidental, consequential or other damages. Our views and rights are the same: You are responsible for your own choices, actions, and results.

Permission should be addressed in writing to Janet & Kathy at janet@storybookpath.com.

Cover Design: Anne Karklins [anne@hasmarkpublishing.com]
Interior Layout: Amit Dey [amit@hasmarkpublishing.com]
Illustrations: Molly Mason

ISBN 13: 978-1-77482-304-0
ISBN 10: 1-77482-304-7

Dedication

We dedicate this book to all who have endured emotional and psychological trauma provided by a prominent caregiver.

We equally dedicate this book to every determined soul who works toward healing, love, peace, happiness and joy along their path.

This is a highly personal, important but difficult story to tell knowing it can make family members uncomfortable.

"Tell your stories," says Anne Lamott, an American novelist and nonfiction writer. *"You own everything that happened to you. If people want you to write warmly about them, they should have behaved better."*

Additionally, we dedicate this book to Molly Mason, its gifted illustrator whose whimsical art and interpretations usher in a spirit of softness and comfort, a perfect balance to a painful story to tell. The brilliant colors and magical detail are delightful and we appreciate her spectacular talents.

Acknowledgements

In gratitude for the unconditional love, encouragement, and support we've received from our **families** ~ those we were born into as well as those we helped create.

In gratitude for our dear **friends** who've been on this writing journey with us, especially those who have continued to coax and cheer us onward for years.

In gratitude for our brilliant **behind-the-scene creative duo**, Kimberly Lauersdorf and Kristan Clark, with candid critiques, enthusiastic readings, and challenging prep-talks.

In gratitude for the **crowd-funding** opportunity through BackerKit, and especially Lafia Morrow's leadership, laughter and navigation of this innovative financial pathway.

In gratitude for the **co-publishing** partnership with Hasmark Publishing International, especially its Founder, Judy O'Beirn's personal buy-in of this project and Jenn Gibson's capable leadership and coordination of their talented team.

In gratitude for the **lived experiences** we write about, because life is definitely not a spectator's sport; and we're proudly battle-tested warriors, now stronger, wiser and more compassionate having traveled these roads.

In gratitude for the **faith and freedom** to be true to ourselves, willing to tell bold stories, the good, the bad and the ugly; truly a legacy project for our culturally-relevant times.

In gratitude to **The Maker of Heaven and Earth, The Divine One** who introduced us to each other as teenagers, so that we could ultimately fulfill our life›s purpose these many decades later, creating works of art and entertainment that will inspire humans forever.

In gratitude of our banner, **Silver Series of Grown-Up Wisdom**, a divine gift that we hold sacred, as we commit to creating and nurturing a genre of those "becoming" and "being" grown-up. It has been said, "it takes a village" to raise a child; and we believe that holds true when raising up "big kids" too. May our thought-provoking, illustrated short stories for grown-ups warm the hearts and minds of our beloved readers, and flourish for many generations.

Ulla's all-time favorite expression is "What the World?!"

One of her earliest childhood memories was a very painful one. Ulla was about four years old. She woke up in the middle of the night, throwing up, sick in her bed. She needed her mommy!

Ulla went to awaken her mother and this is when she came face-to-face with her mom's inner demons, pent-up anger, and uncontrollable rage.

Ulla's mom shouted in a nasty tirade the entire time she was cleaning Ulla up, jerking everything about and changing the soiled sheets. "Don't even think you are getting into bed with me!!"

As Ulla sobbed herself back to sleep after the dreadful experience, she remembered feeling woefully guilty and utterly ashamed. What the World?!

Many, many years later, she found herself growing older and a wee bit wiser. Ulla decided to search for answers to her probing, most relevant life questions:

- ✧ Why am I here?
- ✧ Why are any of us here?
- ✧ What is my purpose?

A self-proclaimed lifelong learner, Ulla decided to deepen her studies and get to the bottom of these questions, once and for all.

So far, she believed her life had been quite ordinary and very similar to the lives of her family members and others in her surrounding community. They all seemed to be living lives of conformity, conforming to people around them.

As far as Ulla was aware, there weren't any great achievers in her family or out in the community, although she carries much love and admiration for every single one of them.

Ulla recognized that many of these people seemed to have self-limiting beliefs surrounding multiple subjects, but the greatest barrier in her own family seemed to be their self-sabotaging thoughts, particularly about money.

They believed wealth was for others, not for them. "Money doesn't grow on trees!" was, by far, their favorite phrase. **"What the World?!"** thought Ulla.

And, falsely, they believed that there was only so much money in the world and that the wealthier folks had "dibs" on it, gobbling it all up and leaving only pennies for the rest of them.

Ulla's mother even sat her down at a very young, formative age and emphatically stated, while pointing her finger toward Ulla's small face, "There are rich people in the world, Ulla, but this is not meant for you."

"What the World!?" Do you know what these negative thoughts can do to a little developing human? They can, and oftentimes do, create emotionally damaging psychological barriers! All life's little lessons and misinformation can go straight into the subconscious mind, our memory, and fester there. And, this can often cause us to grow into conforming, complacent grown-ups.

Unfortunately, little Ulla was raised this way. She didn't have anyone telling her that she could *"be,"* *"do,"* or *"have"* anything she wanted in her life. Sadly, on the contrary, she seemed to be on her own trying to figure that out for herself.

Unfortunately, it often takes many years to unravel the twisted, tangled web of misbeliefs that we weave and buy-in to. And sadly, according to research, less than ten percent (10%) of the population ever figure it out in their lifetime!

For nearly thirty years, Ulla and a group of close friends have regularly met once a month for a little thing they affectionately call "Group Therapy." It all began a long time ago when they played volleyball on the same team, and afterward, would hang out for hours chatting over cocktails.

They would discuss problems in their marriages, their challenges raising children, and other personal subjects.

Most of them blamed others for their shortcomings and failures, but unfortunately, every single one of these ladies had a story of something quite serious that had seemed to impede their emotional subconsciousness.

After all these decades of "Group Therapy," Ruby, Sis, Genevieve, and Ulla have come a long way. But, notably, a fifth member of the group was discreetly removed because she refused to resolve her problems when everyone else was committed to doing the hard work.

Sometimes, people just seem to want to "wallow in their shit," always complaining, bitchin' and moaning. Not only that, but they don't offer any uplifting encouragement for others. With this particular life-sucking cynic, the group determined she would need to be left behind.

Of course, what is discussed in "Group Therapy" always stays in group therapy, but I honestly believe they've covered almost every subject known to humankind through the years. And, it's safe to say that Ruby, Sis, Genevieve, and Ulla have all had their fair share of real "hard knocks" in their lives!

These days, the "Group Therapy" gatherings are mostly fun and filled with lots of joyful laughter. They share a tight bond and are so proud of the progress made through the years together.

Still, Ulla's always searching for "more," and she was determined to set out and conquer all of her self-limiting beliefs. And, perhaps, she's hopeful to step into her best life and fulfill her greatest desires. Honestly, conforming to the beliefs of others felt to Ulla like living in a big cage.

Ulla decided to create her own life on a much less crowded path.

Ulla knew enough to know that ninety-five percent (95%) of people blame others for their failures, not knowing they hold the key to their own success. They believe their own life is shaped by circumstances and external forces of others, and things they cannot control. They are often referred to as, "outward thinking" people.

For many years, Ulla lived her life in much the same way, believing she was shaped by circumstances she couldn't control, living in that big cage mentality.

Her life was based on many predetermined circumstances, like the fact that Ulla's mother and father were expected to get married and have children. They lived in the shadows of a big Catholic church that loomed large, literally and figuratively. The prominent demographic of their neighborhood was people of the German Catholic faith and ancestry, and not surprisingly, both of Ulla's parents were of German Catholic descent.

Within a year and a half of her parents' first wedding anniversary, they welcomed their first child, a precious baby girl.

Ulla was most likely a VERY big surprise, and despite it all, she joined the family exactly seven days before her big sister's first birthday!

Of course, it wasn't Ulla's fault, but by the time she was five, she had become the target of her mother's unleashed anger and uncontrollable, chronic rage. Rather than having a mother's affection lavished upon her, she was exposed to unhealthy "enmeshment" where her narcissistic mother manipulated and controlled many details of her life, often ruling in boundary-breaking behavior.

Instead of being given the building blocks of healthy self-esteem, feeling safe and secure in her place in this world, Ulla learned to internalize a nagging inner critic with a perpetual sense of self-doubt.

Conversely, Ulla's younger brother was her mother's "golden child," and Ulla was often seen as the scapegoat.

Ulla remembers feeling like she was "walking on eggshells" every morning, not knowing what mood she'd find her mother in.

Her mother's emotional and psychological abuse continued well into Ulla's adult years and since her mom had an overwhelming ability to manipulate those around her, Ulla had become, by this time, the "black sheep" of the family.

"The older you get, the dumber you get," Ulla's mother would say to her on a regular basis as she continued to be influenced by her mother's broken wing.

Ulla's mother managed to disinvite her from many family vacations and other events.

To live with any sense of normalcy, Ulla learned to set strong boundaries concerning contact with her mother. Also, her mother's behavior had created an unspeakable wedge between Ulla and her siblings.

And, despite it all, Ulla was able to appreciate loving family members who displayed positive traits. They were her role models and she vowed to follow in their footsteps instead.

Not surprisingly, due to Ulla's emotional and psychological abuse, she has always been fascinated with human behaviors and she read anything she could find on the subject.

Not only did she read about it, but Ulla became a self-proclaimed subject matter expert (SME), observing behaviors surrounding her. This doesn't mean she had gotten to the point of forgiving her mother, as that step would take many more years.

Ulla also studied the power of the mind through the subject of metaphysics. This subject was just as intriguing as the power of forgiveness and the feeling of joy that it brought to Ulla, when she was finally ready to accept it. **"What the World?!?"**

With each new discovery, Ulla felt more connected to Source, self-power, and she grew in a greater self-awareness. It felt so good that she kept going, kept achieving, and searching for the next best thing along her life journey.

Knowing that we are creatures of habit, and having been programmed by others, Ulla also knew enough to know that our minds mostly operate in a negative state.

We become what we think about, and that is another great key to success, but it's also a double-edged sword, and can lead to failure.

Any thoughts of frustration, fear, anxiety, and worry had produced the exact same emotional barrier for Ulla. Instead of reacting with these emotions when something didn't turn out in Ulla's favor, she started asking herself, *"What is here to teach me?"* Or, *"What can I learn from this?"*

The human mind can be compared to a fertile plot of land. You can plant any seed. The earth doesn't care what we plant and neither does the mind. It will produce whatever we plant. "As ye sow, so shall ye reap," says ancient scripture.

Also, according to research, Ulla learned that most of us are operating our minds greatly beneath our ability and the art of setting goals gives us something concrete and worthwhile to work toward.

We don't have to know how we are going to achieve our goals; we only need to leave that up to the Universe.

"What the World!?!" That is the best news yet! We just need to stay in a positive state of mind.

"Oh, crap!" said Ulla, "that's the hardest fucking part!"

However, Ulla Universe was also very familiar with the Laws of Attraction, commonly known as the Laws of the Universe. She'd learned that for every action, we receive an equal or opposite reaction. In other words, if we think positively, we create positive results.

She knew enough to know that she was now "sitting at the wheel" and in the driver's seat of a vast source of energy and she must control her thinking. Now, Ulla set out to think only positive thoughts for the next thirty days.

It was during this time that she stumbled across this quote:

"My mind is the center of Divine operation. The Divine operation is always for expansion and fuller expression, and this means the production of something beyond what has gone before, something entirely new, not included in the past experience, though proceeding out of it by an orderly sequence of growth. Therefore, since the Divine cannot change its inherent nature, it must operate in the same manner with me; consequently, in my own special world, of which I am the center. It will move forward to produce new conditions, always in advance of any that have gone before."

Repetition of good feeling thoughts is one of the keys to help overcome our habitual way of thinking. This is why Ulla made a practice of repeating this quote every morning upon waking and every evening just before falling asleep. She also read her personal **desire (or goals)** and projected date for its arrival while believing the Universe would bring it to her.

During her 30-day challenge, Ulla discovered an inspirational, world-renowned wealth, business, and manifestation expert offering a free online seminar.

This expert, Peggy McColl, talked for two hours about the importance of staying in a positive state of mind and how it can change your life. Interestingly, Peggy had been raised in a poverty-stricken household and early in her life, she thought in only very negative terms.

It wasn't until she was forced to attend a mandatory work seminar given by the late, great Bob Proctor, that her eyes were opened to a new way of thinking. And then, this seminar changed her life!

Ulla knew enough to know that signing up to study with Peggy could only help her on the road to self-actualization. To invest in her continued journey would turn out to be a great gift to herself.

"What the World!?!" Not only did this help Ulla stay in a positive mindset, but she learned how to channel her knowledge and set up multiple sources of income while creating the life she desired.

It was while she was enrolled in Peggy's program that Ulla wrote an entry-level 30-day program so anyone with a pulse could get on their own unique path to finding joy and abundance!

Ulla Universe turned to her "hard knock" life to craft helpful stories of her own lived experiences. Ulla discovered that when we stay true to ourselves, and find an avenue to help others, we will find our life purpose and achieve joy along the way.

Ulla succeeded in her journey to self-actualization; however, this doesn't mean she is perfect and not susceptible to flaws. She is human, after all.

Ulla is also not without problems. She has problems just like everyone else. However, she's learned to solve them with a delicate balance of consideration, class, style, grace, and wisdom.

Ulla practices "Gratification" every single day; another tool for staying in a positive state of mind. This is the practice of consciously expressing gratitude.

Continuing to pursue her life's purpose, Ulla vows to reach new goals and dreams, while simultaneously reaching out and serving others.

Footnote: Adult survivors of complex childhood trauma can struggle with processing what they survived which can lead to emotional and physical symptoms. Equally common are patterns of self-sabotage based on shame and guilt for what they survived. However, we can find building blocks to a life of hope and a better future. By making the most of yourself, you make the world a better place to live.

Give yourself permission to take a new path. All you need is the plan, the road map, and the courage to move forward.

Join the 30-Day,
Entry Level program for Personal Development.

We provide heartfelt, entertaining, real-life stories of adversity about the challenges of overcoming the after-effects endured from psychological and emotional childhood/young adult trauma.

Free Introductory Guidebook, *'OOOH Crap!*
WE BECOME WHAT WE THINK ABOUT'
when you sign up at
WWW.STORYBOOKPATH.COM.

Meet the Authors

Janet Snyder, is the creator of *StoryBookPath.com a 30-day personal development program* and eBook designed to help you discover and live the life you love and desire. After finding her enthusiastic, authentic voice and true strength from her own personal struggle with the negative aftereffects endured from mental and emotional childhood/young adult trauma, Janet's fulfilling her life purpose of helping others.

Also, Founder of *StoryBook Cottages*, she uses her well-earned degree for interior design and her vivacious love of the earth designing playhouses constructed from recycled materials and sustainable living green rooftops. Janet is the mother of three and a "Nan" to her grandchildren who also live in her hometown of Louisville, Kentucky.

Kathleen Canova, successful entrepreneur and founder of the Canova Group, LLC, has facilitated and educated many regarding domestic crisis intervention, including deep emotional and spiritual healing practices. Rooted from her own lived experiences, and after extensive training and certifications, she shares her heartfelt hope, passion and inspiration with humankind.

Living in Westminster, Colorado near her adult children and grandchildren, who affectionately call her "Yaya," she enjoys spending quality time with family and friends when she's not reading, writing and traveling.

Sales Page

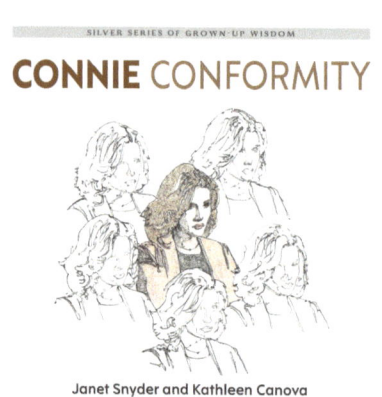

First-Time Co-Authors:

Janet Snyder and Kathleen Canova

Available on Amazon and Ingram-Spark now

www.storybookpath.com

On FACEBOOK: STORYBOOKPATH & SILVER SISTERS WISDOM

janet@storybookpath.com & kathleenkarrercanova@gmail.com